UNOFFICIAL

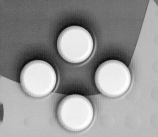

Rocket League
Beginner's Guide

TRAINING
CHALLENGES

Complete the Basic Tutorial in the Training Playlist

Play 1 Online Match

Get 1 Shot on Goal in Online Matches

VIEW CHALLENGES

CREATE PARTY

21st Century Skills **INNOVATION LIBRARY**

Josh Gregory

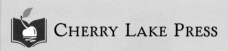
CHERRY LAKE PRESS

Published in the United States of America by Cherry Lake Publishing Group
Ann Arbor, Michigan
www.cherrylakepublishing.com

Reading Adviser: Beth Walker Gambro, MS, Ed., Reading Consultant, Yorkville, IL

Copyright © 2024 by Cherry Lake Publishing Group

All rights reserved. No part of this book may be reproduced or utilized in any form or by any means without written permission from the publisher.

Cherry Lake Press is an imprint of Cherry Lake Publishing Group.

Library of Congress Cataloging-in-Publication Data

Names: Gregory, Josh, author.
Title: Rocket league : beginner's guide / by Josh Gregory.
Description: Ann Arbor, Michigan : Cherry Lake Publishing, [2023] | Series: Unofficial guides. 21st century skills
    innovation library | Includes bibliographical references and index. | Audience: Grades 4-6 | Summary: "Rocket League
    is a big game with a simple idea: what if rocket-powered cars could be used to play soccer? Readers will discover
    how Rocket League went from an indie underdog to one of the biggest games in the world and find out everything
    they need to know to jump in and start competing online. Includes table of contents, author biography, sidebars,
    glossary, index, and informative backmatter"— Provided by publisher.
Identifiers: LCCN 2023002146 (print) | LCCN 2023002147 (ebook) | ISBN 9781668927960 (library binding) |
    ISBN 9781668929018 (paperback) | ISBN 9781668930489 (epub) | ISBN 9781668933442 (kindle edition) |
    ISBN 9781668931967 (pdf)
Subjects: LCSH: Rocket league (Video game)—Juvenile literature.
Classification: LCC GV1469.37 .G747 2023 (print) | LCC GV1469.37 (ebook) | DDC 794.8—dc23/eng/20230126
LC record available at https://lccn.loc.gov/2023002146
LC ebook record available at https://lccn.loc.gov/2023002147

Cherry Lake Publishing Group would like to acknowledge the work of the Partnership for 21st Century Learning,
a Network of Battelle for Kids. Please visit http://www.battelleforkids.org/networks/p21 for more information.

Printed in the United States of America

Note from publisher: Websites change regularly, and their future contents are outside of our control.
Supervise children when conducting any recommended online searches for extended learning opportunities.

Josh Gregory is the author of more than 200 books for kids. He has written about everything from animals to technology to history. A graduate of the University of Missouri–Columbia, he currently lives in Chicago, Illinois.

Contents

CHAPTER 1

A Surprising Success

Sometimes a new video game can seem to come out of nowhere. One minute, you've never heard of it. The next, it's all anyone is playing, streaming, or talking about online. That's what happened when *Rocket League* was released in 2015. Today, it might be hard to imagine a time when this unique, car-based take on soccer wasn't one of the most popular video games on the planet. But believe it or not, *Rocket League* had very humble beginnings.

Rocket League was created by the **developers** at a studio called Psyonix. Psyonix was formed as a small, independent company in 2000. For much of its history, the studio spent most of its time completing projects for larger developers. This means the larger companies would hire Psyonix to complete certain features for big-name, big-budget games. But in between these projects, the developers at Psyonix wanted to create their own games.

In 2008, Psyonix quietly released a game called *Supersonic Acrobatic Rocket-Powered Battle-Cars* as a downloadable title for the PlayStation 3. The concept of the game was simple: players would drive small, rocket-powered cars and use them to try to hit a huge soccer ball into a goal. With little promotion and

Cars and soccer might not seem like a natural combination at first, but after one round of *Rocket League* you'll see that they're a perfect match.

The Work Never Ends

The developers at Psyonix did not stop working on *Rocket League* upon its release. One of the reasons the game has remained popular for so long is that it regularly gets updated with new content and features. The developers have improved the balance of the game by tweaking the way cars and soccer balls move and react to different situations. They have also fixed bugs in the game and added new car types, stadiums, and game modes. These fixes and additions draw in new players and keep old ones coming back to the game. This means the team at Psyonix will likely keep working on the game for as long as people keep playing!

middling review scores from critics, the game was not a huge hit. However, it did find a small audience of devoted fans.

The team at Psyonix knew the main idea of their game was good. They hoped that with a sequel, they might be able to fix some of the problems of the first game and make something that would really catch on. The team started development on the new game in 2013, looking carefully at which features had been popular with players in the first game and which ones were criticized. Eventually, they started inviting players to try out the new game, called *Rocket League*, in online tests. This helped them collect more feedback about what players wanted to see in the game. It also got players talking. Soon, excitement started to grow for *Rocket League*'s release.

Finally, *Rocket League* was released for PC and PlayStation 4 in July 2015. On launch day, it was given away to all subscribers of the PlayStation Plus service as a free download for a limited time. This helped build an audience for the game from day one. As these players enjoyed the game and talked about it with their friends, others got online to buy their own copies.

Rocket League's three-on-three competitive mode was an instant hit with the game's early players.

Meanwhile, the team at Psyonix worked hard to promote their game on social media. Unlike *Battle-Cars*, *Rocket League* received very strong reviews from professional video game critics. This helped increase the hype around the game even more. Within a month of release, there were more than five million *Rocket League* players.

It was clear that the game was a success, and now the pressure was on Psyonix to keep up the momentum.

With both *Fortnite* and *Rocket League* in its lineup, Epic Games has a huge audience of competitive online gamers.

The developers created new versions of the game for the Nintendo Switch and Xbox. This allowed even more people to join in the fun. They also began selling physical copies of the game in stores, instead of requiring players to download it online.

Over time, *Rocket League* only became more and more popular. In 2019, Psyonix was purchased by Epic Games, the company behind games like *Fortnite* and *Gears of War*. It also created the Unreal Engine, a set of **software** tools that developers have used to create many of the most successful games—including *Rocket League*.

Years earlier, when it was still a small, independent company, Psyonix had helped Epic work on some of its biggest releases. But now, thanks to the success of *Rocket League*, Psyonix is no longer a tiny underdog— it's a major development studio and part of one of the biggest gaming companies in the world.

CHAPTER 2

Balls in the Air

Today, it's easier than ever to get started playing *Rocket League*. In September 2020, the game was made free-to-play. This means that anyone can download it and start playing, completely free of charge. All you need is a modern video game console—such as a PlayStation, Xbox, or Nintendo Switch—or a PC with an internet connection. If you have multiple game systems, you can even download the game onto all of them for free and carry your progress from system to system.

When you load up *Rocket League* for the very first time, you'll be treated to a short, exciting intro video. This will lead into a sequence that teaches you the most basic controls of the game: how to **accelerate**, jump, and boost your rocket-powered car. Though there are plenty of other techniques in the game that you'll eventually need to master, these are the basic movements you'll need to get started.

The basic rules of a *Rocket League* match are also very simple. There are two teams—matches can be one-on-one, two-on-two, three-on-three, or four-on-four. The standard is a three-on-three match. Each match is five minutes long. It will begin with a huge soccer ball in the

At the start of each match, both teams race to make first contact with the ball.

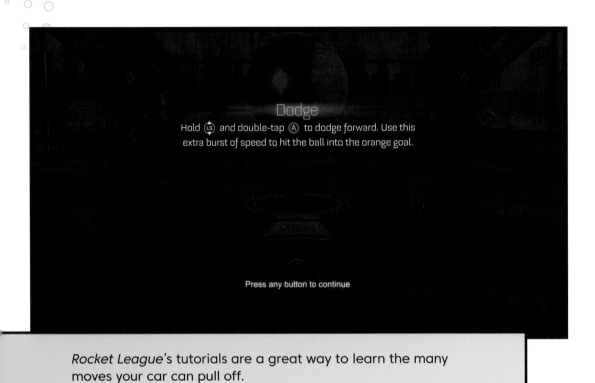

Dodge

Hold (LS) and double-tap (A) to dodge forward. Use this
extra burst of speed to hit the ball into the orange goal.

Press any button to continue

Rocket League's tutorials are a great way to learn the many moves your car can pull off.

center of a field and teams on either side of the ball. Once the timer begins, teams are free to drive around and try to knock the ball into the opposing team's goal. Whichever team has the most goals at the end of five minutes is the winner. If there is a tie, the game will go into sudden death overtime. This means the first team to score will win.

Even though *Rocket League* is pretty simple, playing well is far from easy. You'll need sharp reflexes and a lot of experience to succeed. One good place to begin is with the game's built-in tutorials. To access these, enter Training mode and select tutorials from the menu. You will learn some of the most common techniques and get all the time you need to practice them until you can regularly pull them off without thinking about it.

Playing on the Small Screen

In 2021, Psyonix released a new take on the classic *Rocket League* formula called *Rocket League Sideswipe*. This version of the game allows players to enjoy *Rocket League* action on iOS or Android mobile devices. It's not quite the same game. The action takes place in two dimensions. This means cars can only move up, down, left, and right. But it still has the same basic gameplay of classic *Rocket League*, with two teams competing to score goals by using their cars to knock a soccer ball around.

Once you feel pretty comfortable with the basics of operating your car, try jumping into a match with other players. You can either play split screen mode with real-life friends in the same room or go online to play with millions of others around the world.

As you play your first few matches, concentrate on keeping track of the ball's location. Arrows around your car will show you which direction the ball is in when it's not visible onscreen. And when the ball is in the air, you'll see a target on the ground showing where it is

Backspace Reset Ball
1 Take Possession
2 Start Dribble
3 Pass Ball
4 Launch Ball
5 Defend Shot

PRESS SPACEBAR TO TOGGLE

100

When you turn on the Ball Cam, the game's camera will stay locked on the ball no matter which way your car is facing.

When the ball is in the air, keep a close eye on the circle on the ground to help you figure out where it will land.

going to land. You should also try to keep an eye on your opponents' locations. And as you move around the soccer field, try to collect the glowing boost items. These will come in handy for pulling off advanced techniques. All of this is probably a lot to keep track of at first. But as you keep playing, everything will start to feel like second nature.

CHAPTER 3

Scoring Goals

Rocket League is the kind of game where it is easy to learn the basics, but very tough to master at a high level. When you first start playing or watching streams, you'll see players doing things that look downright impossible. When you take the controls yourself, you might wonder how you could ever play that well. Don't get discouraged. Almost everyone feels this way when they start playing *Rocket League*. It takes a whole lot of practice to truly get good at the game. But in the meantime, there are some tricks and moves you can use to help improve your odds.

When you are starting out, your instinct might be to chase after the ball as it gets knocked around the field. But instead, try playing more carefully. Think about the positions of your car, your teammates, your opponents, the ball, and the goals. Don't cluster up with your teammates. Try to be in the right spot so that when the ball pops out from a cluster of players you can hit it toward the opponents' goal or away from your own.

Sometimes players will cluster around the goal, making it hard for anyone to get a clean shot.

You might also try to use your speed boost as often as you can when you are still learning how to play. Instead, practice saving it for just the right moments. A short burst of speed to get ahead of an opponent or reach the ball before it gets to your goal is more useful than zipping around the field constantly.

Time your speed boosts just right to reach the ball before opponents.

Backspace Reset Ball
1 Take Possession
2 Start Dribble
3 Pass Ball
4 Launch Ball
5 Defend Shot

You can get a lot of height with a simple double jump.

As early as possible, try learning all the different moves you can do with your car. There is a lot more than just driving and jumping. Using the powerslide allows you to turn sharply. This is very important when the ball gets behind you during a match. You'll also want to learn all the ways of getting your car into the air.

You can perform a double jump by jumping again once you are already in the air. Even more exciting is to try boosting once you're in the air. If you do it correctly, your car can fly for a short distance. This can really come in handy when the ball is bouncing around. It's tough to control at first, though, so you'll need plenty of practice.

Tap to jump. Pitch up with S. Hold to fly. Rocket fly to hit the balls onto the ground.

Learning to control your car while rocket boosting in midair is tough at first, but it will give you an advantage over opponents.

Riding up the sides of the arena can help you get a better angle for your shots.

It probably didn't take you long to realize that you can drive your car right up the walls of the arena during a match. If you have enough speed, you can even get all the way onto the ceiling before you fall off. This can be a great way to quickly get from one side of the arena to the other. If you time it right, you can even get the drop on your opponents by hitting a flying ball as you fall from the ceiling!

One helpful thing you can do to contribute in any match is to play defensively. If you aren't sure how to help your team, simply position yourself in front of your own goal. Any time the ball heads your way, knock it back toward the opponents' side of the field. It's not the flashiest way to play, but if you do it right you can make a big difference in the outcome of a match.

Esports Excitement

As *Rocket League*'s popularity took off during the early days after launch, players quickly realized that it would make a perfect game for esports competitions. The game was immediately popular on Twitch and other streaming services. The simple concept makes it easy for viewers to follow the action, and it's a lot of fun to watch.

In 2016, Psyonix began hosting its own annual tournament called *Rocket League* Championship Series. In the first year, it offered $55,000 in prizes. Today, the prize money is much higher, with each tournament offering more than two million dollars. *Rocket League* has also become an important part of other major esports organizations, including Major League Gaming and ESL.

Scoring a goal is always the main objective, but there are also many other ways to help your team to victory.

Just be sure not to accidentally knock the ball into your own goal—it will count as a goal for the other team!

Working together with your teammates is an important part of *Rocket League*. This is easiest when playing with the same group of friends regularly. You can practice strategies together and learn each other's play styles. You can also use voice chat as you play. But even when playing with a group of strangers and no voice chat,

Opening the quick chat menu will let you choose from some basic phrases you can use to coordinate plans with teammates.

Good teamwork will lead to victory.

you can still be a good team player. Don't crash your car into your teammates, and don't be a ball hog. For example, try to set up your teammates to score by knocking the ball into their path. Just like in real soccer, passing frequently is a great way to score goals!

CHAPTER 4

Custom Cars

Like most of today's other popular online games, *Rocket League* offers players all kinds of ways to express their creativity with unlockable **cosmetic** items. Some can be unlocked by completing special challenges and playing well in matches, which will earn players points called XP. Collecting XP allows players to level up their Rocket Pass. With each new level in the Rocket Pass, new cosmetic items are unlocked and added to the player's garage. This is where they can go to customize their cars.

There are two versions of the Rocket Pass: a free one and a paid one. The paid version offers more items than the free one. It also increases the rate at which players gain XP, making it easier to level up.

Players can also buy cosmetic items directly from an in-game store. Each purchase is a **microtransaction** costing a relatively small amount. Some items are only in the store for a limited time, and the store's current offerings change each day.

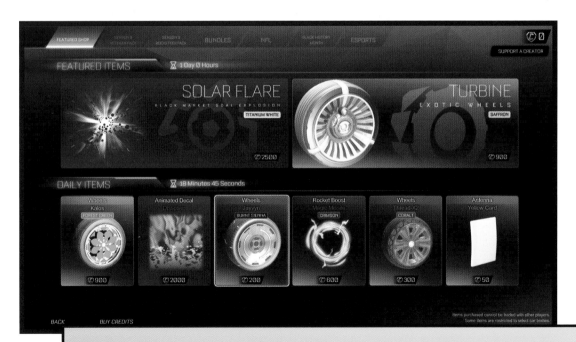

Rocket League's in-game store allows players to purchase a wide variety of cosmetic items.

You can also unlock cosmetics for free by leveling up the Rocket Pass. To do this, simply play games and do your best to win.

To access all the cosmetic items you've unlocked and use them to customize your car, select "Garage" from the main menu. Here, cosmetics are organized into several categories. First off is the car's body, or general shape. This is probably the biggest change you can make to a car's appearance. It is also the only kind of cosmetic that has any effect on gameplay—the shape of your car makes very small differences in how it can connect with the ball.

Next, you can choose to add decals to your car, such as flames or skulls. After that, you can choose the colors of your car, as well as the finish of the paint. In other words, do you want your car to be shiny? Dull? Wood-textured? It's all up to you.

Express your creativity when you're choosing an appearance for your car. Every player's car will look different.

You can also change your car's wheels and the design of the blasts that come out of your car's tailpipes when boosting. Toppers are decorative objects that sit on top of your car, while antennas stick up from the side of the car. Goal explosions are exactly what they sound like—the type of explosion that occurs when you knock a ball into your opponents' goal. Trails are the types of sparks that come off your car's tires when zipping around. Finally, engine audio allows you to change what your car sounds like as it drives around.

Spending Wisely

Collecting new cosmetics and customizing your car can be a lot of fun. But it can also be expensive if you aren't careful. Even though each microtransaction might only cost a small amount, these amounts can quickly add up.

Talk to a parent or guardian before you spend money in *Rocket League* or other games. Ask about setting up a budget. Then be sure to stick to it—don't spend more money than you agreed. And remember that spending more will not help you win. Only practice and skill can help you with that!

BALL CAM
PRESS Ⓐ TO TOGGLE

A topper can be anything from a tiny cactus
to a giant sombrero.

If this all sounds like a lot to keep track of, that's
because it is! *Rocket League* has tons and tons of
options for customizing your car, so you can create
something truly unique. Pick something that suits you,
then get out there and start scoring some goals!

GLOSSARY

accelerate (ak-SELL-uh-rayt) increase in speed

balance (BAL-uhns) the overall difficulty level and fairness of a video game's various systems and rules

bugs (BUHGS) errors in a computer program's code

cosmetic (kahz-MEH-tik) relating to how something looks

developers (dih-VEL-uh-purz) people who make video games or other computer programs

esports (EE-sports) organized, professional video game competitions

microtransaction (MYE-kroh-trans-ak-shuhn) something that can be purchased for a small amount of money within a video game or other computer program

software (SAWFT-wair) computer programs

FIND OUT MORE

Books

Gregory, Josh. *Careers in Esports*. Ann Arbor, MI: Cherry Lake Publishing, 2021.

Loh-Hagan, Virginia. *Video Games. In the Know: Influencers and Trends.* Ann Arbor, MI: 45th Parallel Press, 2021.

Orr, Tamra. *Video Sharing. Global Citizens: Social Media.* Ann Arbor, MI: Cherry Lake Press, 2019.

Reeves, Diane Lindsey. *Do You Like Getting Creative? Career Clues for Kids.* Ann Arbor, MI: Cherry Lake Press, 2023.

Websites

With an adult, learn more online with these suggested searches.

Rocket League

The official *Rocket League* home page is a great source for the latest news and updates about the game.

Rocket League Wiki

Check out this fan-made website for highly detailed, in-depth info about every aspect of *Rocket League*.

INDEX